Longhouse

Written by
Cynthia Breslin Beres

Illustrated by
Kimberly L. Dawson Kurnizki

The Rourke Book Company, Inc.
Vero Beach, Florida 32964

For our Jordan Rose

© 2001 The Rourke Book Company, Inc.

Printed in the United States of America

Library of Congress Cataloging-in-Publication Data

Beres, Cynthia Breslin, 1953-
 Longhouse / Cynthia Breslin Beres.
   p. cm. — (Native American homes)
 Includes bibliographical references and index.
 Summary: Describes the way of life of the tribes that made up the League of the Iroquois, focusing on their longhouses, unique dwellings built for shelter and ceremonies.
 ISBN 1-55916-247-3
 1. Longhouses—Juvenile literature. 2. Iroquois Indians—Juvenile literature. [1. Longhouses. 2. Iroquois Indians—Dwellings. 3. Indians of North America—Dwellings.] I. Title. II. Series.

E99.I7 B47 2000
392'.36'00899755—dc21

00-027815

Printed in the USA

Contents

3

The Land of the Iroquois

The Iroquois people were farmers, hunters, and traders. They lived in woodlands that stretched from the southern Great Lakes into the St. Lawrence River Valley. Later, this land became part of New York State and eastern Canada.

The land of the Iroquois had many streams, rivers, and lakes. These were home to fish, ducks, geese, and beaver. Rolling hills dropped down into green valleys that were ideal for growing corn. All around were thick forests filled with deer, bear, and other wildlife.

Winters were very cold. Rivers, lakes, and even the earth froze under heavy snow. In spring the land thawed, and the Iroquois could plant crops. Summers were hot, with just enough rainfall to help crops grow tall. The cool days of autumn brought the end of the growing season.

The Iroquois tribes who lived in this land called themselves the "people of the longhouse." The name came from the houses of wood and bark in which they lived.

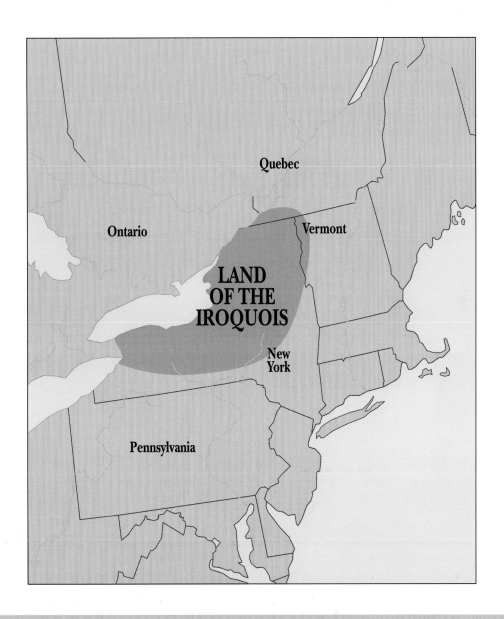

Quebec

Ontario

Vermont

LAND
OF THE
IROQUOIS

New
York

Pennsylvania

The Iroquois Tribes

The Iroquois were really five different Indian tribes, or nations: the Mohawk, Oneida, Onondaga, Seneca, and Cayuga. They all spoke languages that sounded alike, but they had no form of writing.

More than 500 years ago, the five tribes agreed to live in peace. They formed the League of Five Nations. Later, a sixth Indian nation, the Tuscarora, joined. These six tribes became the League of the Iroquois. Together they fought off raids by their common enemy, the Ojibwa tribe.

A path called the Iroquois Trail connected the tribes of the League. Warriors from different villages met along this trail. They traded food and supplies and shared news.

Once a year, the League of the Iroquois held its great council meeting in a special *ceremonial* longhouse. Each tribe had certain jobs at the meeting. The Mohawks and Senecas watched the doors. The Oneidas and Cayugas kept the hearth fires burning. The Onondagas ran the meeting.

The Longhouse

The longhouse was a large wooden building covered with bark. Longhouses were 30 to 200 feet (9 to 61 meters) long and from 15 to 25 feet (5 to 8 meters) high. Big longhouses could hold as many as 100 people at a time. Some longhouses were longer than a football field!

Longhouses were built facing in different directions. This made it hard for flames to jump from house to house when there was a fire.

The families in each longhouse were related through their women. These families were all part of the same family group or clan. Girls and boys born into the same clan were sisters and brothers.

An Iroquois village had many longhouses and many clans. A large clan might fill many longhouses in one village. Each clan named itself for an animal spirit such as bear, turtle, hawk, and wolf. The oldest woman in each clan was in charge of their food supply. She also picked men to speak for the clan at village council meetings.

Trees for the Longhouse

It took careful planning—and many trees—to build a longhouse. Iroquois men and boys could cut young trees down easily. These were used to frame the house.

However, it took many hours to chop down a big tree. First, the men packed a ring of clay around the tree trunk, a few feet off the ground. Then they piled dry branches against the trunk below the ring and set them on fire. The clay ring stopped the fire from spreading up the tree. The men then chopped into the burned trunk below the ring with stone-headed axes. This work had to be repeated many times before the tree finally came crashing down.

Bark was peeled from the big trees in large sheets or slabs up to 8 feet (2.5 meters) long. The men wet these slabs to keep them from cracking. They were then stacked on top of one another. The men placed logs or large rocks on top of each stack to make the slabs dry flat.

Building the Longhouse

Building a longhouse took many days. Men and boys first cleared the land of trees and brush. Then they marked an outline of the house on the ground. The men placed *vertical* poles in holes dug all along the outline. These formed the outer frame of the house. They then tied *horizontal* poles around the frame using bark strips.

Boys climbed to the tops of the vertical poles. They tied more poles across the top of the frame to hold it together. Rows of lighter poles were then stretched across the house to support the roof. The poles were bent toward one another and tied together where their ends crossed. This formed the roof's peak or arch.

Once the longhouse was framed, women and girls helped attach the bark walls. They stretched the dried bark slabs on the ground in a long row. Then they punched holes through the top of each slab with sharp *awls* made of bone. They slipped bark cords through these holes and strung the slabs together in long sheets.

The sheets were then placed against the outside of the longhouse. The men tied them to the frame, starting at a bottom corner of the house. They worked sideways, then upward. Each layer of bark slightly overlapped the one below. The overlap allowed rainwater to run off and prevented leaks. The men tied another set of poles around the outside of the house to keep the bark walls from blowing off in strong winds. Finally, they covered the roof with bark shingles tied into place with bark cord.

The Iroquois often decorated the outside walls of the finished longhouse with red and black pictures of animals, birds, and people. A *symbol* of a clan's animal spirit, called its totem, might also be painted. Clan members hung carved wooden totems over the doorways that led into their new longhouse.

Inside the Longhouse

The Iroquois built each longhouse with two doorways, one at each end. They covered these openings with deer hides or bark slabs on wooden hinges. Each door opened first into

Inside a modern-day replica of an Iroquois longhouse.

a small room where the women stored extra food and supplies for winter. In summer, the bark walls of these rooms were taken down to make front and back porches.

In the main part of the longhouse, a wide passage or aisle ran down the center from end to end. All along this aisle were fire pits used for cooking and heat. In the roof above each fire pit was a smoke hole. Sunlight from the smoke holes lit up the inside. There were no windows. The longhouse had a dirt floor.

Two or three wooden platforms ran like shelves along the inside walls of the longhouse. The Iroquois used these platforms for working, sitting, sleeping, and storage. The women hung clothing, tools, and weapons from wooden poles above the platforms. They braided corn together by the husks and hung the corn from poles. They also hung strings of dried apples, pumpkin, and squash from poles. Dried fish and meat were hung over the fire pits to keep them safe from mice and dogs.

Each family in the clan had its own room or compartment along one wall of the longhouse.

Compartments were
about 12 feet (3.5 meters) long
and 6 feet (1.8 meters) wide. They were
separated from one another by bark walls or
partitions for privacy. Women covered their
sleeping platforms with bark mats and with
mattresses and pillows stuffed with old corn
cobs. They piled fur blankets on top for warmth.
Each family had a storage shelf. Here they kept
snowshoes, weapons, hunting gear, and other
items. The women stored cooking pots, carved
spoons, and water bowls beneath the families'
sleeping platforms.

Each family shared a cooking fire in the center of the aisle with the family across the way. As many as twelve family fire pits were located along the aisle. Clan members gathered around their fire pits to eat and to visit with each other.

A Home for All Seasons

The Iroquois lived in their longhouses year-round. However, they spent much of their time outdoors. In winter, they kept warm by the longhouse fires and ate dried meats and other foods. When it rained, they used wooden poles to pull bark slabs partway over the smoke holes from inside the house. This stopped the rain from pouring in. The air inside the longhouse would become smoky and hard to breathe. Lying down on a sleeping platform was the best way to escape the smoke.

In spring, the men and women cleared the land for crops. Women then planted Indian corn or maize, beans, and squash. The Iroquois called these crops the "three sisters."

In summer, the longhouse was much less crowded. Men and boys were out hunting and fishing or trading with other tribes. Women and girls tended the crops and cared for older family members and young children.

In the fall, the Iroquois *harvested* their crops. They stocked food and supplies for winter.

Iroquois Villages

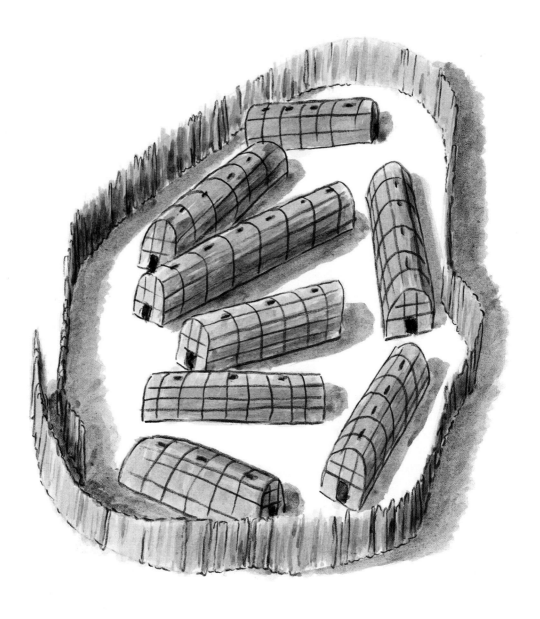

The Iroquois settled in villages near their fields. Villages were built on flat hilltops high enough to spot enemy war parties. They were also located close to fresh water and firewood.

Iroquois villages had from 12 to 200 longhouses. As many as 1,000 people might live in one village. Each village was surrounded by a tall wooden wall called a stockade. The stockade protected the village from enemy raids. It was made of thick tree trunks tied together with bark ropes. The stockade had watchtowers and only one entrance to prevent surprise attacks.

The Iroquois moved out of their old villages every ten to twenty years. By then, the soil in the fields was worn out from farming, and the supplies of wood were used up. After many years, longhouses became very dirty. Ceilings were covered with black *soot* from the fires. Mice and insects were a problem, too.

A new village was built close to the old one. The Iroquois did not tear down their old longhouses when they moved. They were left behind to fall into *ruin*.

Special Longhouses

An important part of each Iroquois village was the ceremonial longhouse. Council meetings were held here. The Iroquois also performed plays, songs, and dances, such as the Eagle Dance, in the ceremonial longhouse. Festivals were held to thank the good spirits and to chase away evil ones.

In modern times, the tribes of the Iroquois League still hold their great council meetings in

ceremonial longhouses. Today's special longhouses are not like the old longhouses. They are built with human-made materials and tools. Many have chimneys, glass windows, kitchens, and furniture.

Over the years, *archaeologists* have discovered evidence of the old Iroquois villages and longhouses. These archaeological sites tell many things about how the Iroquois people lived so long ago. They are like open classrooms and often can be visited by the public.

The Iroquois Longhouse Today

In 1535, Jacques Cartier, a French explorer, was the first European to meet the Iroquois. Soon traders, missionaries, and settlers came.

In 1930, skilled Iroquois workmen perched high above the city as they bolted together the steel beams that framed New York's Empire State Building.

Contact with these Europeans brought fighting, new sicknesses, and destruction to the Iroquois. They struggled to survive. The Iroquois had to change the way they lived.

In the early 1900's, men from the Mohawk tribe became skilled at building big-city *skyscrapers*, such as New York City's Empire State Building. Nicknamed "sky walkers," they worked on narrow steel beams perched more than a thousand feet above busy city streets. This work called for sharp eyesight, steady balance, courage, and much teamwork. These are all qualities for which the Iroquois are known.

Today the people of the longhouse live in modern houses. Many live on *reservations* in New York State and eastern Canada. Few bark longhouses are built, and they are mostly museums. The old Iroquois Trail is now Interstate Highway 90. Each day, it carries thousands of cars and people through the ancient land of the Iroquois.

Make a Model Longhouse

What you will need:

a shoebox (no lid)
one large piece of thin cardboard
twigs or small sticks
brown felt or other fabric
glue
scissors
red and black fabric paint (in squeeze bottles)

To make your longhouse:

1. Start with the open side of the shoebox facing up. Cut a door at each end of the house with scissors. Glue twigs and sticks around the box.

2. Cut two small pieces of brown fabric and glue them over the doorways. Decorate the walls of the longhouse with red and black paint. Paint an animal totem over each door.

3. Make a rectangle with the thin piece of cardboard for the roof. Fold the cardboard in half the long way and cut out 3 or 4 smoke holes along the crease. Open and glue or tape the roof to the top of the longhouse.

Glossary

archaeologist: a person who studies the way humans once lived, using objects found in the ground such as bones and pottery; an *archaeological site* is a place being studied.

awl: a sharp sewing needle carved from bone.

ceremony: a celebration with special activities and meanings; a *ceremonial* longhouse was used for these activities.

harvest: to gather food from plants and crops.

horizontal: parallel to the ground.

reservation: a piece of land set aside for use only by Native Americans.

ruin: fallen apart; wrecked.

skyscraper: a building made of steel, glass, and concrete or stone that is so tall it seems to touch the sky.

soot: a black powder that comes from burning fire.

symbol: a mark or picture that means something.

vertical: upright.

Further Reading

Banks, Lynne Reid. *The Indian in the Cupboard*. New York: Avon Camelot, 1980.

Hofsinde, Robert. *Indians at Home*. New York: William Morrow, 1964.

Monroe, Jean Guard, and Ray A. Williamson. *First Houses: Native American Homes and Sacred Structures*. Boston: Houghton Mifflin, 1993.

Ridington, Jillian, and Robin Ridington. *People of the Longhouse*. Buffalo, N.Y.: Firefly Books, 1995.

Shemi, Bonnie. *Houses of Bark*. Plattsburgh, N.Y.: Tundra Books, 1990.

Wolfson, Evelyn. *The Iroquois*. Brookfield, Conn.: Millbrook Press, 1992.

31

Suggested Web Sites

The First Americans
<www.germantown.k12.il.us/html/intro.html>
Native America (native lore; animal totems)
<www2.itexas.net/~sparrow/native.htm>
Mythology of North American Indians
<msgc.engin.umich.edu/cgi-bin/tour>
American Indians and the Natural World
<www.clpgh.org/cmnh/exhibits/north-south-east-west/index.html>
Search Engine Source
<www/yahooligans.com/School_Bell/So...Studies/Cultures/Native_Americans/Tribes>

Index

Photo credits: Cover, p. 16, Ben Klaffke; p. 26, Lewis Hine/ National Archives.